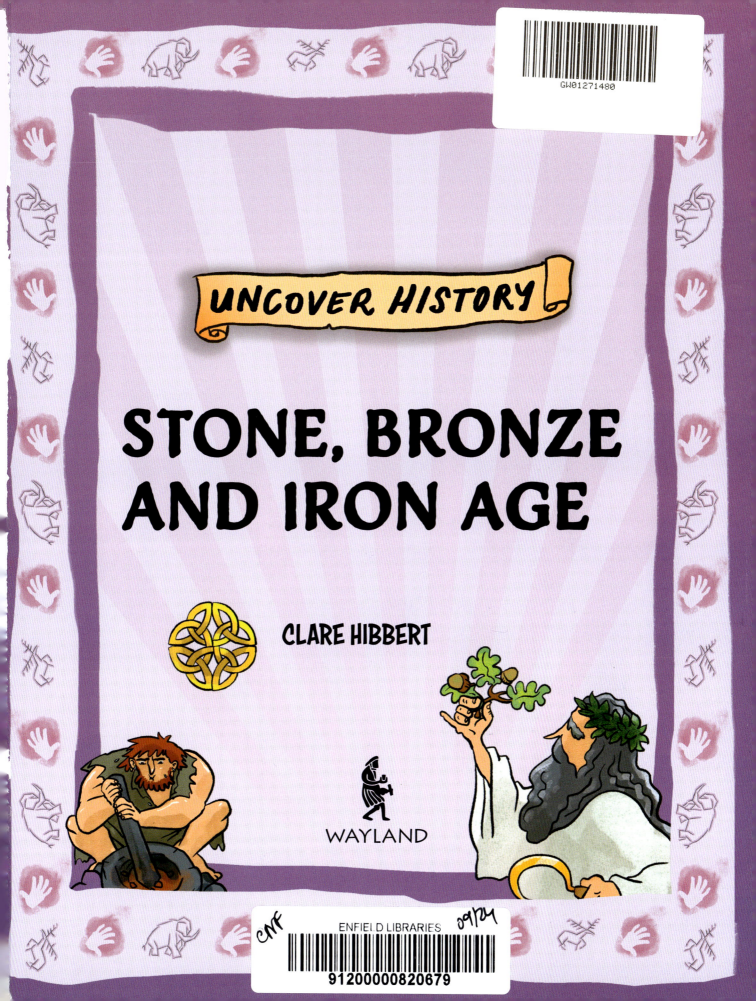

UNCOVER HISTORY

STONE, BRONZE AND IRON AGE

CLARE HIBBERT

WAYLAND

First published in Great Britain in 2023 by Hodder & Stoughton

Copyright © Hodder & Stoughton Limited, 2023

All rights reserved.

Series Editor: Lisa Edwards
Series Design and illustration: Collaborate

The text in this book first appeared
in *History Detective Investigates: Stone, Bronze and Iron Age* by
Clare Hibbert (Wayland).

HB ISBN: 978 1 5263 2214 2
PB ISBN: 978 1 5263 2215 9

Printed in Dubai

Wayland
An imprint of
Hachette Children's Group
Part of Hodder & Stoughton
Carmelite House
50 Victoria Embankment
London EC4Y 0DZ

An Hachette UK Company
www.hachette.co.uk

MIX
Paper from
responsible sources
FSC® C104740

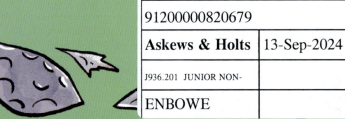

London Borough of Enfield	
91200000820679	
Askews & Holts	13-Sep-2024
J936.201 JUNIOR NON-	
ENBOWE	

CONTENTS

Who were the first Britons? 4
When was the Middle Stone Age? 6
What did people do in the New Stone Age? 8
What were Stone Age tombs like? 10
Why was Stonehenge built? 12
When did the Bronze Age begin? 14
Who were the Beaker people? 16
When did people learn to make iron? 18
What were Iron Age homes like? 20
Who were the Celts? 22
What did the Celts believe in? 24
How did the Iron Age end? 26
What to do next 28
Glossary 30
Find out more 31
Index 32

Who were the first Britons?

Early humans reached Britain at least 800,000 years ago. They may have belonged to a species called *Homo erectus*, which had spread across Europe and Asia from Africa.

Today, there is only one kind of human on earth – *Homo sapiens*. But before we came along, there were many different human species. *Homo erectus* evolved in Africa 1.8 million years ago and was able to make simple stone tools. The period *Homo erectus* lived in is known as the Old Stone Age.

Best rock … EVER!

Hunter-gatherers crossed the wide land bridge that still connected Britain to Europe. They followed herds of animals, from deer to mammoths and woolly rhinos, and killed them for their meat and skins.

Bagsy the big hairy one at the front!

Who wants to hold the fire first?

Me! Me!

At night, people made rough shelters or slept in caves. They had fire, but probably couldn't start one. Instead, they found smouldering branches after lightning strikes or wildfires and kept them burning.

When Was the Middle Stone Age?

The period from about 11,500 to 6,000 years ago is known as the Middle Stone Age. People led more settled lives. They cleared woodlands and built sturdier shelters, where they would stay for a few months at a time.

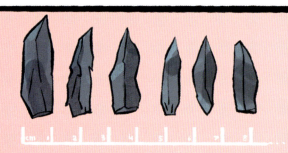

They crafted tiny, sharp flint blades called microliths. They made bows and arrows for shooting birds, and nets and baskets for catching fish and shellfish. They made dugout canoes for paddling.

They had domesticated (tamed) dogs, which enabled them to hunt animals such as deer, elk and wild boar. These people had better tools than their predecessors. They used spear throwers, devices that fired spears farther.

Music was an important part of people's lives. They kept time in ritual dances with drums and flutes. At Star Carr in Yorkshire, archaeologists have discovered more than twenty masks or headdresses made from deer skulls. Shamans probably wore these during rituals to enter a trance and come closer to the animals or the spirit world.

Middle Stone Age people may have been cannibals. There are strange cuts in the human skulls and other bones found in Gough's Cave in Cheddar Gorge. Maybe they were victims – sacrifices to keep the gods happy.

"I hope you're happy now!"

Another theory is that their brains had been eaten by the living, thinking it would allow their ancestors' spirits to live on. Some skulls were shaped into cups, which were probably used to hold blood, wine or food.

"If you don't eat your brains, you're not getting any pudding"

What did people do in the New Stone Age?

People in Britain took up farming in the New Stone Age (around 4000 to 2400 BCE). They cleared trees with polished stone axes and planted crops, bringing seeds from mainland Europe.

Farming had begun about 11,500 years ago in Egypt and Mesopotamia (ancient Iraq). Over thousands of years, farming skills spread west through Europe.

They said just to plant the seeds and wait ...

Great! I'm *literally* starving!

People learned how to sow, harvest and store crops.
They also brought over sheep and cows, and tamed native wild boar into pigs.

Only two houses? Our village has FOUR!

Farmers didn't need to move around, tracking animals. They could stay in one place. New Stone Age farmers lived in villages, building homes from timber and stone.

One of the best-preserved New Stone Age villages is Skara Brae on Orkney Mainland, which was inhabited from about 3200 to 2500 BCE. Its eight houses were built sunk into the ground to protect against the cold. Their roofs had whalebone or timber frames and were covered with moss or turf.

Just think of the dough we'll make!

People spent a lot of time farming and preparing food. Grinding grain to make flour for bread was back-breaking work.

People still made hand axes and other tools from stone and bone, but they became fussier about their materials.

In places where there was good-quality flint, people dug mines. These mines were dangerous places.

Please let me find the best piece of flint ever!

Please let me find a piece of flint better than Greg's.

Sometimes one shaft was kept as a shrine, where people could make offerings to the gods. They might have asked to be kept safe or for luck finding good stones. Miners traded their flint for other goods.

What were Stone Age tombs like?

In their settled villages, New Stone Age people began to take more care over how they buried their dead. They dug underground tombs and marked burial sites with dolmens, mounds or barrows.

Dolmens consisted of a few huge stone slabs that supported a flat stone, known as the capstone. People erected dolmens all over Europe and the British Isles.

Well, stone me, it's huge!

Not all dolmens have human remains under them. The ones that were not tombs might have been put up as markers to show that a particular family lived on and farmed that area of land.

One of the grandest mounds is the one at Newgrange in County Meath, Ireland. Built about 3200 BCE, it measures 76 m (250 ft) across and has a wall running round the edge. A passage leads to a central chamber, which has smaller chambers leading off it.

Newgrange was probably used for special ceremonies. It was designed so that at dawn on the winter solstice, a beam of sunlight shone through an opening above the entrance and lit up the main chamber. New Stone Age people must have understood how the position of the Sun in relation to the Earth changed over a year.

Barrows were simple mounds, covering just one burial chamber.
Long barrows, named for their oval or rectangular shape, might cover a group of tombs.

Silbury Hill is the tallest human-made mound in Europe (40 m (131 ft) high) It would have taken a team of 500 workers about 10 years to build.

Why was Stonehenge built?

Stonehenge is Britain's most famous prehistoric site. However, exactly why the circle of standing stones was erected and how it was used remain a mystery.

Over the years, people have suggested that the monument might have been a temple, a burial site, a healing centre or even a kind of calendar.

- Bluestone horseshoe
- Circle of bluestones
- Circle of sarsen stones
- Sarsen horseshoe

"Which way is June?"

Stonehenge was built in stages over about a thousand years. The first stage began around 3000 BCE, when people dug a circular ditch and bank. This kind of earthwork is called a henge. Small pits inside the henge were dug to bury people's ashes after they had been cremated. Some of these pits contain grave goods.

There are two types of stone at Stonehenge. The smaller ones, known as bluestones, went up around 2600 BCE. They came from the Preseli Hills in south-west Wales more than 250 km (156 miles) away.

"Cheer up! Only another 249 km to go!"

They were probably transported using rafts along rivers and rollers on land. The larger stones, known as sarsen stones, were dragged from the Marlborough Downs using sledges and ropes. Each weighed about 25 tonnes.

The stones at Stonehenge were carefully positioned. At dawn on the summer solstice, the sun rose to the north-east of the circle. At midwinter, the sun set in the south-west, between the gap in the central horseshoe.

When did the Bronze Age begin?

The Bronze Age was the period of history when people began to make things out of metal. In Britain, it started around 2500 BCE. But the first metal that people learned to work was actually copper, not bronze.

Metal usually has to be extracted from metal-rich rock, called ore, which is found underground. Metalworkers crushed the copper ore using a mortar and pestle. Then they heated it over a fire to melt the metal – a process known as smelting.

I feel like I'm smelting already!

For an arrow escape!

Finally, they poured the molten metal into moulds. To make copper arrowheads, for example, metalworkers used arrowhead-shaped clay moulds.

After people had learned to shape copper, they began to use tin and gold. By about 2150 BCE, they discovered that copper and tin could be mixed to make a stronger metal: bronze. To feed the demand for bronze, more mines opened up.

There were large copper mines at Great Orme in North Wales and in Ireland at Ross Island, County Kerry and Mount Gabriel, County Cork. There were tin mines in Cornwall and Devon.

Metals were used for useful objects, such as tools and containers, and also for display objects. People could show off their high status by wearing fine brooches and bracelets. The most ornate pieces were made of sheet metal that was hammered into shape as it was cooling. The spectacular golden cape discovered at Mold in Wales was made of sheet gold.

Who were the Beaker people?

The Beaker people appeared in western Europe around 2800 BCE. They made tools, weapons and jewellery, also often found in their burials. They traded the objects they made and their culture spread.

The Beaker people are named after the bell-shaped beakers they also made, which were decorated with lines. Their beakers were used to hold mead (a honey drink) and beer, food, metal ore and even human ashes.

A man known as the Amesbury Archer was buried with five Beaker pots near Stonehenge around 2300 BCE. There were also clothes, tools and weapons. By examining his DNA, scientists discovered that the Amesbury Archer had grown up in the Swiss Alps.

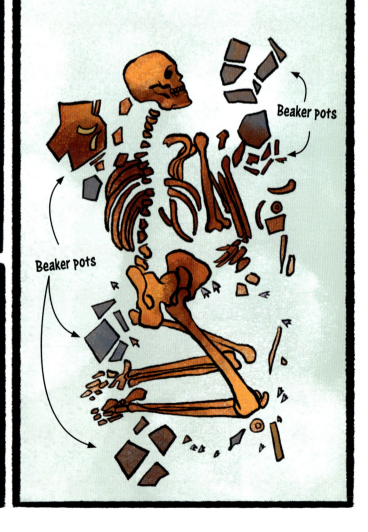

Beaker pots

Beaker pots

Beaker culture only flourished in Britain until about 1700 BCE, but trade links with Europe continued. A wooden boat discovered near Dover dates to the 1500s BCE. Made of oak planks, it would have been used to ferry tin, bronze and other goods across the English Channel.

Horses were becoming an important means of transport during the Bronze Age. They could pull farm carts and were also useful in warfare, carrying horseback warriors or drawing war chariots.

I said 'CHARGE!', not 'Chill'!

It better be, or I'm ditching these guys.

This is going to be our last ditch attempt.

As the Bronze Age continued, there was increasing violence in Britain. Chiefs grew rich and powerful through trade or mining, and fights over territory and resources became common. To protect themselves from raids, people built defensive ditches around their villages.

When did people learn to make iron?

The first iron objects were made in Britain about 1000 BCE, and by 800 BCE iron had become the main metal being worked. This date marks the start of the Iron Age.

Iron ore was more common than copper or tin so it was easier to find, but the metal itself was harder to extract. It needed hotter temperatures and, often, repeated heating and hammering.

Within a few hundred years, most tools in Britain were made of iron, and this led to an amazing increase in food production. Using iron axes, farmers could clear greater numbers of trees; with iron shovels and ploughs they could cultivate heavier soils.

They were sowing improved varieties of barley and wheat that yielded bigger harvests. Farmers also planted more peas, beans, flax and other crops.

Iron Age people did not just change the landscape through farming. They also built nearly 3,000 hill forts across Britain. These were hilltop settlements, protected by ditches and banks.

Some hill forts were only used as a safe refuge in time of war but others like Maiden Castle in Dorset were fortified towns where people lived all the time. They were packed with roundhouses, barns for livestock, granaries, forges and textile workshops. The marketplace sold local produce, as well as pottery, wine, oil and glassware imported from Europe.

What were Iron Age homes like?

Most Iron Age homes were roundhouses.
Some had timber frames and wattle-and-daub walls.
Others were built from stone. Roofs were thatched or covered with turf.

Inside the home, there was just one circular room. At the centre was the hearth fire. There was no chimney, but a lot of the smoke escaped naturally through the thatch. The fire heated and lit the home and was used for cooking, too.

Some households had metal cauldrons that could be hung over the fire from a three-legged metal stand. Alongside the fire there was often a small clay oven for baking bread.

When women weren't cooking, grinding grain into flour or helping with the garden or livestock, they wove wool to make warm clothes for all the family. At night the family slept on hay mattresses, under wool blankets and animal skins.

In Scotland, people built brochs – circular stone towers, up to four storeys high. These may have been lookout posts, surrounded by smaller roundhouses.

Scottish wheelhouses were stone buildings with spoke-like walls that divided the space into rooms. The largest were about 11.5 m (37.5 ft) across and housed several families.

Who were the Celts?

'Celts' is the name given to lots of scattered tribes that existed across Europe during the Iron Age, including the 'Britons' who settled in Britain in about 600 BCE.

The Britons were made up of about 30 different tribes, including the Iceni of eastern England. They all spoke similar languages and shared similar customs. They wore fearsome 'war paint' – blue dye extracted from a plant called woad.

"Come on! Let's go get 'em!"

"One sec, I just want to get this contouring right."

golden torc

bronze helmet

The Celts lived in tribal communities where everyone had family ties, and answered to a warrior chief or king. They were successful farmers and their craftworkers produced beautiful metalwork, pottery and jewellery.

Archaeologists have unearthed many hoards of Celtic treasure – gold and silver coins, torcs (neck rings), bracelets, shields, daggers and swords. Some were buried in times of danger for protection and others were offerings to the gods.

Celtic burials can often be hard for archaeologists to find, but hundreds have been discovered in Yorkshire. The most spectacular are the twenty or so chariot burials, where individuals were buried with their chariots, including a woman.

Bodies preserved in peat bogs tell us a lot about Iron Age people. Clonycavan Man from Ireland and Lindow Man from Cheshire were both in their twenties, both victims of ritual murders and both were wealthy. Exactly why they were killed is a mystery, but it may have been to please the gods.

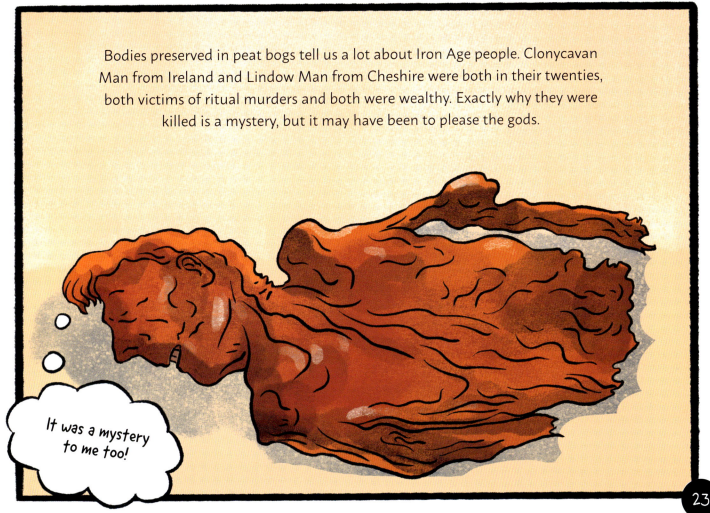

It was a mystery to me too!

What Did the Celts Believe In?

Just as there was no single people called the Celts, there was no single set of Celtic beliefs. However, certain practices and gods were common among many or all tribes.

The Celts worshipped hundreds of gods. Some looked after an aspect of the world, such as light, dawn or thunder. Some were in charge of a particular area of human existence, for example motherhood, warfare or the afterlife. Several gods were associated with more than one idea.

As farmers, the Celts made offerings to certain gods in the hope that they would bring times of plenty. Sucellus was a god of farming, thunder and forests, who woke up the earth each spring by striking it with his hammer. Cernunnos, an ancient god who had stag's antlers, was another provider, frequently shown feeding animals.

The Celts also believed in countless minor gods, who inhabited particular rocks, trees, rivers, lakes or mountains. People gave gifts to these gods, throwing bronze or gold armour into rivers and burying precious jewellery in the earth. They also tossed offerings into waterfalls, wells and springs, because they thought these places were doors from this world into the next.

Wow! My favourite!

The Celts believed that everyone who died went to an afterlife. Oak groves (small woods) were sacred to the Celts, and they performed special rituals there.

Blessings on this house.

They also worshipped in small household shrines as well as larger temples. Roman authors say that priests called druids carried out rituals to help guarantee the people's safety and prosperity.

How did the Iron Age end?

In Britain, the Iron Age ended when the Romans arrived, bringing their customs with them and changing the British landscape with their roads, towns, forts, villas and farms. Celtic culture slowly merged with Roman ideas and practices.

Julius Caesar was the first Roman general to invade Britain in 55 BCE. Tribes in southern Britain drove him off, and although he returned the following year with more men, he was not able to capture the island. The Emperor Augustus planned an invasion in 34 BCE, but had to call it off because of trouble elsewhere in the empire.

That's the last we'll see of them!

Although they did not rule Britain, the Romans were still able to get their hands on its rich resources, thanks to strong trading links. But in the 40s CE, the Romans were worried that conflicts among Celts were threatening their supplies of resources such as tin and wool. So in 43 CE, Emperor Claudius sent his troops to subdue Britain.

What to do next

Now you've learnt all these facts about the Stone Age, Bronze Age and Iron Age, why not try and discover even more? Using this book and other sources.

1. Make your own 'Ice Age' engravings by scratching animal outlines onto old pieces of bone or wood – find out what wild animals lived in your country during the Stone Age.

2. Recreate a prehistoric cave painting using the information you've gathered about the wild animals or reproduce a Celtic pattern on an old T-shirt using clothes dye.

3. Create your own 'henge' or dolmen stone monuments using modelling clay or real stones and use lamps to recreate the solstice shining through them.

4

Imagine you are part of Boudicca's Iceni tribe army, preparing to meet the Roman troops. Write a diary of the morning before battle.

5

Draw an aerial plan of an Iron Age hill fort. Label the most important features.

6

For your research, use the Internet and your local or school library. Look and see if your local museum has any prehistoric collections.

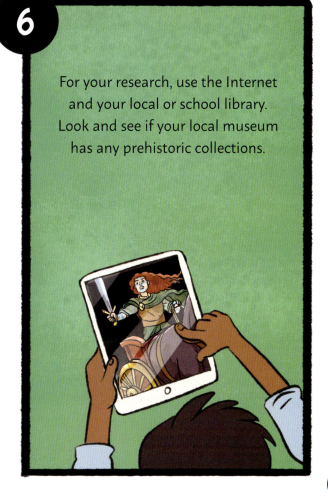

GLOSSARY

archaeologist Someone who studies the remains of past societies.

barrow A large mound, often built to mark a burial site.

barter To trade by swapping goods, not using money.

BCE 'Before the Common Era'. Used to signify years before the believed birth of Jesus, around 2,000 years ago.

Beaker A culture and people in western Europe during the early Bronze Age.

Bronze Age The period when people learned to work metal. In Britain, it lasted from around 2500 to 800 BCE.

CE 'Common Era'. Used to signify years since the believed birth of Jesus.

dolmen A Neolithic monument, where a flat stone rests on some upright stones, often built to mark a grave.

druid A Celtic priest.

evolution The process by which living things change over long periods of time and may give rise to new species.

flint A very hard stone.

grave goods Objects placed in tombs for use in the afterlife.

hand axe A cutting tool made from flint, which fits in the hand.

henge A circular ditch and bank of earth built as a monument, sometimes topped with standing stones or wooden pillars.

hill fort A hilltop fortified by defensive ditches and banks.

hoard Buried treasure.

hunter-gatherer Someone who lives by hunting, fishing and collecting wild foods.

ice age A period when the climate is so cold that ice sheets cover the ground.

Iron Age The period of history when people learned to work iron. In Britain, it lasted from around 800 BCE until the Romans arrived in 43 CE. In Ireland, it lasted until around 400 CE.

Middle Stone Age The period when people were hunter-gatherers using advanced stone tools. In Britain, it lasted from around 9500 to 4000 BCE. Also known as the Mesolithic Age.

New Stone Age The period when people began to farm. In Britain, it lasted from around 4000 to 2500 BCE. Also known as the Neolithic Age.

Old Stone Age The period when people used simple tools of stone, wood and bone. In Britain, it lasted from around 800,000 to 11,500 years ago. Also known as the Paleolithic Age.

prehistory The time before written records. In Britain, prehistory ended with the arrival of the Romans in 43 CE.

shaman A tribesperson believed to be in contact with the spirit world.

solstice Midsummer or midwinter. In Britain, which is in the northern half of the world, these fall on 21 June and 22 December.

wattle-and-daub a material used in building walls, consisting of interwoven sticks and twigs covered with mud or clay

Find out more:

Books to read

The Celts (The History Detective Investigates) by Philip Steele (Wayland, 2011)

Early People (Eyewitness) (Dorling Kindersley, 2003)

Prehistoric Britain by Alex Firth (Usborne, 2010)

The Secrets of Stonehenge by Mick Manning and Brita Granström (Frances Lincoln, 2013)

Websites

www.stonepages.com

www.bbc.co.uk/wales/celts/

www.mustfarm.com

Places to visit:

British Museum, London WC1B 3DG

Creswell Crags, near Worksop S80 3LH

Flag Fen, Peterborough PE6 7QJ

Stonehenge, near Salisbury SP4 7DE

Note to parents and teachers:
Every effort has been made by the publishers to ensure that these websites are suitable for children. However, because of the nature of the Internet, it is impossible to guarantee that the contents of these sites will not be altered. We strongly advise that Internet access is supervised by a responsible adult.

INDEX

Amesbury Archer 16
Avebury 11, 13
barrows 10, 11
Beaker culture 14, 16
bog people 23
Boudicca 27
Bronze Age 14-15, 16-17, 18
burials 5, 10-11, 12, 16, 23, 26
Caesar, Julius 19, 26
cannibalism 7, 25
carvings 2, 29
Celts 22-23, 24-25, 26, 27
Cernunnos 24
chariots 17, 23
Cheddar Gorge 7
chiefs 17, 29, 22, 23
copper 14, 18
dolmens 10
druids 25
farming 8, 9, 10, 17, 18, 22, 24, 26
fire 4, 5, 14, 20
gods 7, 9, 22, 23, 24-25, 26
Great Orme 14
hand axes 5, 8, 9
henges 12, 13

hill forts 18, 19, 27, 28
homes 6, 8, 19, 20-21, 20, 21
Homo erectus 4
Homo heidelbergensis 5
Homo neanderthalensis 5
Homo sapiens 4, 5
horses 2, 17, 24
Iceni 22, 27
Iron Age 18-19, 20-21, 22-23, 24-25, 26-27
Maiden Castle 18, 18, 19
metalworking 14, 15, 16, 18, 19, 22
Middle Stone Age 6-7, 6
mining 9, 14
Mold cape 15
New Stone Age 8-9, 10-11, 12-13
Newgrange 10, 11
Old Stone Age 4-5
rituals 6, 6, 7, 23, 25, 25
Romans 19, 22, 25, 26-27, 28
roundhouses 19, 20, 21
Silbury Hill 11
Skara Brae 8, 8
solstices 11, 12
standing stones 11, 12, 13, 28

Stonehenge 12-13, 12, 16
tin 14, 16, 18, 19, 27
tools 4, 5, 6, 9, 14, 15, 16, 18
torcs 22, 25
trade 9, 16, 17, 19, 26
tribes 22, 23, 24, 26, 27
wheelhouses 21